Infinite
WORTH

Cover and interior design by Christina Marcano
Cover design copyright © 2016 by Covenant Communications, Inc.
All images from iStockPhotography.com.

Published by Covenant Communications, Inc.
American Fork, Utah

Printed in Hong Kong
First Printing: October 2016

22 21 20 19 18 17 16   10 9 8 7 6 5 4 3 2 1

ISBN-13:978-1-52440-113-9

Infinite WORTH

Seeing Yourself
through the Eyes
of the Master

TONI SORENSON

Are you ready to face the truth—the whole truth, and nothing but the truth—about yourself? Are you serious about forging an eternal relationship with Christ? Are you passionate about living the gospel to its fullest? Are you really ready to live the life Christ lived and died for you to have? *If you are, then it's time you let Christ—and no one else—define you.*

Trials are not signs that you are unloved or unlovable. Adversity refines and **STRENGTHENS US.** It's not allowed into our lives to ruin us. It's there to make us stronger, more substantial **IN EVERY WAY.**

See yourself
as God sees you:
as His child—
a child of infinite worth,
one who is
loved
beyond measure.

Everyone on this earth struggles—even those who seem to have all the advantages. It's part of God's plan. **It's how we come to the realization that we have to rely on Him instead of on our own strength.** And it brings us to a realization of His merciful plan. Regardless of any disadvantage we face, our Heavenly Father can fill any void and can make up for all that we lack. **He knows us better than we know ourselves,** and His perfect plan can catch us when we fall and redeem us when we sell ourselves short.

How can we really get to know this celestial Father whose perfect love never fails? How do we begin to identify ourselves as His children? *We find Him on our knees.*

Study all you can about the Great Parent of the universe. Try with all your heart to keep His commandments; repent when you don't. **SPEND TIME WITH HIM.** Serve Him. Most of all, plead that through the Holy Spirit, you might understand your true identity and infinite worth. For above all that God has done, He has created you.

And above everything that God is, He is your Father.

Simply by virtue of being a **CHILD OF GOD,** you are loved with a love that is beyond comprehension, **a love without boundaries or conditions.** You are a child of God, who created worlds without number—and of all those creations, **you are at the pinnacle.**

You were entrusted to come to the earth in these last days to do again what you did before—to once again choose good over evil. You have come into the world at a **most significant time.** We are entering the final stages of a great war. This war commenced before the foundations of the world and has been pursued with awful consequence throughout the world's history. While God's kingdom has been established on the earth in times past, the people to whom the kingdom was previously committed were unable to keep it. This time, however, is different. The prophetic promise is that **this time God's kingdom will not be lost, but will overcome the world.**

"Remember the worth of souls is great in the sight of God" (D&C 18:10). We are not told to learn that the worth of souls is great in the sight of God. We are not told to **UNDERSTAND**. We are told to **remember**. That can mean only one thing: *at some point we knew our worth in the sight of God.*

Imagine how fast our

HEAVENLY FATHER WHIPS

AROUND and comes to our aid

when He hears us cry out to Him!

He is mindful of us—of what is

going on in our lives.

He wants to hear from us,

and **He wants to help.**

Our Father in Heaven
and our Savior stand ready to
CHEER US ON,
to pick us up when we fall,
and to carry us across
the finish line
if we've worn ourselves out in
the cause of the kingdom.

No human mind can fully grasp **the gift of Christ's Atonement,** the vastness and inclusiveness of the act—but in the end, it comes down to just you and Jesus. You've come, and He's met you with open arms—**and now it's just between the two of you.** As C. S. Lewis wrote, "[God] has infinite attention to spare for each one of us. He does not have to deal with us in the mass. You are as much alone with Him as if you were the only being He had ever created. When Christ died, **HE DIED FOR YOU INDIVIDUALLY** just as much as if you had been the only man [or woman] in the world" (*Mere Christianity* [1943], 131).

Jesus extended to us the invitation, **"Come, follow me,"** that we might know what it is like to live in peace and freedom from sin—in joy along the journey. And Jesus died for us so we might come unto Him.

He begs us to take advantage of His Atonement.

The most important message
of all lies in knowing
that we are loved by our
Father in Heaven
and by His Son, our Savior.
There is no more
powerful headline,
no greater news to broadcast.

What does Christ think of you? With all your sins and all your flaws, you are deemed deserving of divine love. **Christ stands ready to make up for all that you lack.** His Atonement doesn't just cover your sins, **IT CONSOLES YOUR SUFFERING.**

This is the Savior's invitation: "Look unto me in every thought; doubt not, fear not" (D&C 6:36). That scripture speaks to us saying that if we're looking to the Savior, **THINKING AS HE THINKS, THEN THERE IS NO ROOM FOR SELF-DOUBT AND NO SPACE FOR FEAR.** There is no scale where one person weighs in more valuable than another. Feelings of depression and inadequacy do nothing but destroy—and God's work is about building, not destroying.

Discover **all you can** about
your Savior. Test His word.
Allow Him to carry the burdens that
buckle your knees. **HAVE FAITH**
in what He says—so much faith that
you go out and do what He did.
Use the force of
Christ's Atonement.

God is going to win in the end, but

we can **choose** to win now.

We can define the quality

of our lives **BY RELYING ON**

CHRIST FIRST, LAST,

AND ALWAYS.

With God,

there is

always

HOPE.

Stay on the Lord's side and you're **guaranteed** a victory, because our Heavenly Father is greater and **has greater POWER** than anything Satan is or anything he has.

If your days seem dark, even when the sun shines for the rest of the world, take heart in what Elder Jeffrey R. Holland taught: that even if you can't always see the "silver lining" in your clouds, **your Heavenly Father can,** and He will match your tears with *His own as He provides the light you are seeking.*

You were born into this life.
equipped to succeed. You are a
part of God's perfect plan.
Yes, you.
The plan would not be perfect
if you were missing.
Think about that.
**You matter more than
you know.**

Together is another word we have to camp on. Our Father has given us agency. It is one of His great gifts to us. He will never force us to refine our lives. He will work with us and through us. The choice will always be ours. **But the result will be His. We must work TOGETHER.**

One of God's greatest gifts to us is the joy of **trying again,** for no failure ever need be final. That's because our Loving Father in Heaven has put Jesus Christ in charge. The plan they set forth **for us is perfect.** That's doesn't mean we are perfect, but it does mean that we . . . have inherited the **POTENTIAL TO BECOME LIKE HIM.**

Our trials in life are not meant to harm us, **but to help raise us up.** We knew before agreeing to come to earth that we would face adversity here *but that we would not be left alone.* Christ has agreed to be with us **"ALWAYS."**

With Christ, it's not about our past, **but our future.** He wants us to learn from our mistakes, to live the best we can, and to HOPE

FOR A BRIGHT TOMORROW.

No matter how bleak your circumstances, **no matter who you were in the past,** no matter what you're going through in the present, **GOD CAN REPAIR YOUR LIFE,** *He can restore your joy.*

Why is it that we tend to **measure our worst** against someone else's best? Doing so makes it difficult to understand the leniency and love with which Jesus judges us. Keeping our focus on the Savior keeps our focus off ourselves. It allows us to be more aware, more grateful, more positive, and even more humble. **IT ALLOWS US TO BECOME OUR STRONGEST, BEST SELVES.**

The most destructive thing we can possibly do in life is to make another person **doubt his worth and identity as a CHILD OF GOD.** The very most productive thing we can do is to help ourselves and others realize that as *children of God, our worth is infinite.*

CHRIST

alone has the **right**
to define us.
His is the defining voice that
we should believe
and heed.

No relationship is **more important** than the one we forge with our Savior, because it determines the relationship **we have with ourselves.** Those relationships are built through the **defining moments of our lives.**

Are you aware of who you really are in relationship to the very God who created the Universe, who scattered the stars and aligned the planets? **Only to those who remember and realize that they are literally spirit children of a God who knows and**

LOVES THEM, can the fire of refinement be welcome. Otherwise, pain and adversity are just that: pain and adversity. Without that knowledge, the refining fire won't purify—it will only burn.

No matter who you are or where you are, no matter what you've done or what's been done to you, Jesus knows and is ready and **ANXIOUS TO LOVE YOU** and to redeem you. **It's all part of a plan that we agreed to,** a glorious but simple two-part plan that cannot fail if we do our part—because *Jesus Christ will never fail to do His.*

Jesus is our Mediator for the Father. **HE IS OUR ADVOCATE.** Until we realize that, we cannot begin to understand the love that accompanies the **refining process** through which we must all go. Until then, all we feel is suffering, and who wants to be grateful for pain?

Every single person born into this world, without exception, has come embedded with a light—**THE LIGHT OF CHRIST.** That light helps us make the choices that *will lead us home.*

GOD CAN see in you what others—even you— cannot. He knows that you have worth. He knows that you have potential. And he knows with His grace and mercy, with **His refining Atonement** burning brightly, fire will not destroy you, but will purify and **MAKE WHAT SEEMED SO IMPOSSIBLE POSSIBLE.**

Life can be brutal. It's not meant to be fair, and it isn't. But when the fire grows too hot and the acid burns too deep, you can call out to the Refiner and He will answer. At some point *you will be able to see His image shining in your countenance,* and that is when you'll know that the refining process is working

AND IS WORTH IT ALL.

Jesus Christ is our Savior.
He is not some distant god who is quick and harsh to punish. The Savior is involved, patient, and "mighty to save" (2 Nephi 31:19). There is no overestimating the value of Christ in our lives. It's **His voice** that needs to be the **DEFINITIVE VOICE TO WHICH WE LISTEN.**

The Atonement seems like it happened so long ago, but in a very real sense our part of that great plan happens **every time we call out for Jesus to save us,** **every time we "come unto Christ,"** whenever we renew our covenants, whenever we **TRULY REPENT** and offer as our part a **broken heart and a contrite spirit.**

Heavenly Father didn't send us to earth blindfolded with our memories erased, expecting us to grope around in darkness and hopelessness. He sent us with everything we need to find our way back to

Him, with everything we need to become like Him. He promises us His help, and He is the only one in this life who will never let us down or disappoint us. He always keeps His promises.

Christ, above all, knows just how hard life can be. *Christ, above all, knows just how high we are capable of soaring* when the impurities of mortality no longer weigh us down. Can you feel the heat of refinement burning within you? It's the fire that will make you pure and **mold you into something useful and valuable.**

God would not have **sacrificed**

HIS SON to save us if these two

principles were not true:

(1) We need saving; and

(2) We are worth saving.

Jesus provided **Himself as our SAVIOR.** Our part is to allow Him to save us. When we do all we can, **He helps carry our burdens—He succors us.** He is infinitely able to do that, because He has personally experienced all of it, *even our darkest hours.*

Christ never fails us, but because we are mortal, we are going to fail Him from time to time. When we do, **we have to believe**— not in our own failing, but in His goodness, His compassion, and His mercy. This great plan in which **WE ARE TAKING PART IS A PLAN OF HOPE.**

Every single one of the people I deem most Christlike has weathered great adversity. Every single one of them. As Elder Neal A. Maxwell observed, if our souls were marked by rings, as are trees, **the years of greatest personal growth would likely be those characterized by the greatest moisture**—*not as the result of rainfall, but of tears* (see Neal A. Maxwell, "Thanks Be to God," *Ensign*, July 1982, 51).

"There is no habit, no addiction, no rebellion, no transgression, no apostasy, no crime exempted **from the promise of complete forgiveness.** That is the promise of the **ATONEMENT OF CHRIST.**"
—President Boyd K. Packer

In this life there is a plan in place—a perfect plan designed by our Heavenly Father to assure our safe return, but also to ensure that we have the opportunity of a life in mortality that is filled with learning and growth. A Cherokee saying says it all: "When you were born, you cried and the world rejoiced. Live your life so that when you die, **the world cries and you rejoice.**"

God has equipped you with **everything you need to build an ideal life,** but you will have to be daring. You're going to have to dare to stand alone, dare to be different, dare to reach out, and dare to be the one who lifts someone else. You can't be complacent or conform if you want to be an **INSTRUMENT IN BUILDING GOD'S KINGDOM.**

Your Heavenly Father knows the pain you are going through. His Son stands ready to heal you everywhere you hurt. But you have to come to Him. **YOU HAVE TO ASK, TO KNOCK, TO SEEK.** As Dr. Martin Luther King advised, "Take the first step in faith. *You don't have to see the whole staircase, just take the first step.*"

Don't just come to the Savior when you're in pain and suffering. **Show up at the throne of grace when your day is filled with sunshine and your HEART IS POUNDING WITH GRATITUDE.**

The relationship you develop with God will be **the most important relationship** you can possibly cultivate. This is the very purpose of the refining process: *to develop spirituality.*

You are called to something great because you are **capable of greatness.** You have the personality, the intellect, the will, and the support to do whatever that "great" feat is. President Gordon B. Hinckley counseled, "Believe in yourself, my brothers and sisters. You are a child of God. **You do have something of divinity within you. Believe in your capacity to DO GREAT AND GOOD THINGS.**"